The Bush Theatre and The Royal Lyceum Theatre Company, Edinburgh,
present

The Girl With Red Hair

By Sharman Macdonald

hampstead theatre

23 March – 16 April

ROYAL
LYCEUM
THEATRE
COMPANY
thebushtheatre

Cast

(In order of appearance)

Stuart	**Christopher Dunne**
Cath	**Patricia Kerrigan**
Izzy	**Helen McAlpine**
Corrine	**Emma Campbell Jones**
Matt	**Sean Biggerstaff**
Sadie	**Sandra Voe**
Ina	**Sheila Reid**
Pam	**Joanne Cummins**

Director	**Mike Bradwell**
Designer	**Robin Don**
Lighting Design	**Gerry Jenkinson**
Sound Design	**Tom Zwitserlood**
Assistant Director	**Jemima Levick**
Deputy Stage Manager	**Heather Wilson**
Production Manager	**Felix Davies**
Company Stage Manager	**Ros Terry**
Wardrobe Supervisor	**Rebecca Morrison**

Press Representation	**Alexandra Gammie**
	020 7833 2627

Graphic Design	**Emma Cooke, Stem Design**

The performance runs for approximately 90 minutes with no interval

The Girl With Red Hair was commissioned by The Bush Theatre and received its world premiere at The Royal Lyceum Theatre, Edinburgh, on 19th February 2005

Christopher Dunne Stuart

Theatre credits include *Baby Jeannie* (BAC), *The Informer* (Kings Head), *Translations* (Manchester Contact), *Battle of Aughrim* (BAC & Tour), *Playboy of The Western World* (Birmingham Rep), *A Bright Light Shining* (Bush Theatre), *Boots for the Footless* (Tricycle), *The Shaughraun* (RNT), *The Shadow of the Glen* (Gate Theatre), *Land of Hope and Glory Boys* (Durham Theatre) and *Progeny* (Belfast Arts Festival).

Television credits include *The Bill* (Thames), *Colourblind* (Tyne Tees), *Night of the Campaign* (BBC), *Land of Hope and Glory Boys* (Tyne Tees), *Crossfire* (BBC), *Shoot to Kill* (Yorkshire TV), *Parnell* (BBC), *Bergerac* (BBC), *The Nations Health* (Euston Films), *Sorry* (BBC), *Minder* (Euston Films), *People to People* (Channel 4) and *Anything More Would be Greedy* (Anglia).

Film credits include *Irish Jam* (Irish Jam Films), *The Notebook of Cornellus Crow* (Perspective Pictures), *Conspiracy of Silence* (Littlewing Films), *28 Days Later* (DNA Films), *Lighthouse* (Winchester Films), *Wired* (Lighthouse Productions) and *Eat The Peach* (Strongbow Productions).

Patricia Kerrigan Cath

Theatre credits include *The Crucible* (Birmingham Rep/Tour), *Top Girls* (Citizens Theatre), *Mr Nobody* (Soho Theatre), *Falling* and *Shang-a-Lang* (Bush Theatre), *King Lear* (Shakespeare's Globe Theatre), *The Memory of Water* (National Tour), *Abandonment* (Traverse Theatre), *The Storm* (Almeida Theatre), *Macbeth* (Bristol & Tour), *Beautiful Thing* (Bush Theatre), *Love's Labour's Lost* and *Women Laughing* (Royal Exchange Theatre), *The Duchess of Malfi* and *All's Well That Ends Well* (RSC), *Schism in England* (National Studio), *Carthaginians* (Hampstead Theatre), *Twelfth Night* and *Le Cid* (Cheek By Jowl).

Television credits include *Silent Witness*, *Doctors*, *Where the Heart Is*, *Dalziel and Pascoe*, *Casualty*, *Macbeth*, *Bright Hair*, *The Crow Road*, *Flowers of the Forest*, *Medics Series III & IV*, *Ghosts*, *A Skirt Through History*, *Sherlock Holmes*, *Age of Treason*, *Dr Finlay's Casebook*, *A Fatal Inversion*, *Taggart*, *Boon*, *Shrinks*, *Playing for Real* and *Imaginary Friends*.

Film credits include *To Kill a King*, *The Magic Toyshop*, *Dancing*, *Joyriders* and *The Find*.

Helen McAlpine Izzy

Theatre credits include *Peter Pan* (MacRoberts), *Fierce* (National Tour/Grid Iron), *Dr Korczak's Example*, *King Matt* (TAG Theatre), *Word for Word* (Magnetic North), *The Happy Prince* (MacRoberts), *The Good Woman of Setzuan* (TAG Theatre), *Farm Land* (Grey Coast Theatre) and *Blooded* (Boilerhouse). Theatre credits at Queen Margaret University College, Edinburgh, include *An Experiment with an Airpump*, *Tartuffe*, *Into the Woods*, *The House of Bernarda Alba* and *Cider with Rosie*.

Television credits include *Cracked* (STV), *Intergalactic Kitchen* (BBC), *Stacey Stone* (BBC), *The Angry Brigade* (BBC) and *Fire, Burn – Taggart* (STV).

Radio credits include *Taglines* (Tag/BBC).

Emma Campbell Jones Corrine

Emma graduated from Central School of Speech and Drama in 2004.

Theatre credits at the Central School of Speech and Drama include *Love Is Disgusting*, *Mephisto*, *Vassa Zheleznova*, *The Kitchen*, *Richard III*, *The Way of the World*, *All My Sons*, *A Midsummer Night's Dream* and *Phillistines*. Other theatre credits include *Pfunk* (Offbeat Theatre Company), *A Small Affair* (Artists Theatre School) and a tour of *Pride and Prejudice* (Good Company).

Sean Biggerstaff Matt

Theatre credits with Scottish Youth Theatre include *Beauty and The Beast*, *Two Weeks with the Queen*, *Hamlet*, *Much Ado About Nothing*, *The Peter Pan Man*, *Sleeping Beauty* and *Macbeth*. Other theatre credits include *Macbeth* (Tron Theatre/Dundee Rep).

Film and television credits include *Charles II* (BBC), *Cashback* (short film), *Harry Potter and The Chamber of Secrets*, *Harry Potter and The Philosophers Stone* (dir. Chris Columbus), *The Winter Guest* (dir. Alan Rickman) and *The Crow Road* (dir. Gavin Miller).

Sandra Voe Sadie

Sandra trained at Edinburgh College of Speech and Drama (now Queen Margaret University College).

Theatre credits include *Home* (Oxford Stage Company), *Playhouse Creatures* (West Yorkshire Playhouse), *Camera Obscura* (Almeida and Apollo), Mistress Quickly in *Henry V*, *Henry IV*, *parts 1 & 2* and The Nurse in *Romeo and Juliet* (all for The RSC), *Attempts on her Life* (Royal Court at The Ambassadors), *A Delicate Balance* (Nottingham Playhouse), *The Winter Guest* (West Yorkshire Playhouse/Almeida), *The Kitchen* (Royal Court), *The Deep Blue Sea* (Almeida), *Medea* (Royal Exchange), *Saturday Sunday Morning* (Birmingham Rep), *The Birthday Party* (Shared Experience), *Dona Rosita* (Bristol Old Vic), *One Woman Show* (tour of Shetland Isles), *The Strangeness of Others* (National Theatre), *Gin Trap* (Bush), *Maria Marten* (Crucible, Sheffield), *Blisters* (Bush and tour), *The Government Inspector* (Crucible, Sheffield), *The Seagull* (Almeida and tour), *Mother Courage* (Pheonix Theatre, Leicester), *The Comedy Without Title* (Lyric Hammersmith and tour), *Daughter In Law* (Hampstead), *Three Sisters* (Bloomsbury and Tour), *Hedda Gabler* (Haymarket) and a one-of with Simon McBurney and John Berger for Artangel, *The Vertical Line*.

Television credits include *Holby City*, *Monarch of The Glen*, *Foyle's War*, *Playing the Field*, *Kid in the Corner*, *Real Women II*, *Great Expectations*, *Holding On*, *The Hello Girls*, *Bare necessities*, *Body and Soul*, *The Crying Game*, *Love Hurts*, *Uncle Vanya*, *Changing Step*, *Look Me in the Eye*, *Stepping Out*, *Donal and Sally*, *Bread or Blood*, *Brother to the Ox*, *Across the Water*, *Gates of Gold*, *The Practice*, *Silent Twins*, *Picture Friend*, *YES*, *The Refuge*, *Knowing The Score*, *Past Caring*, *Open All Hours*, *Coppers*, *Secret Dreams Beautiful Lies* and *Victoria Wood Special*.

Film credits include *Vera Drake*, *Breaking the Waves*, *Hidden Flaws*, *Janice Beard 45WPM*, *Felicia's Journey*, *Drifting*, *The Winter Guest*, *Immortal Beloved*, *Naked*, *Salt on our Skin*, *Erik the Viking*, *Comrades*, *Local Hero*, *The Ploughman's Lunch* and *Agatha*.

Sheila Reid Ina

Sheila is a founder member of The Actors Company. Theatre includes seven years with Olivier's National Theatre including *The Beaux' Stategem, Three Sisters, The Crucible, Hedda Gabler, Othello* (also film). Other theatre credits include *Romeo and Juliet, The Virtuoso, 'Tis Pity She's a Whore, Richard III* (RSC), *The Gentle Avalanche* (Most Promising Actress Award), *My Mother Said I Never Should, Black Milk, Terrorism* (Royal Court), *One Flea Spare, The Marshalling Yard* (Bush), *When I Was a Girl I Used to Scream and Shout* (Bush, Edinburgh Lyceum and Whitehall, Olivier Nomination), *The Importance of Being Earnest* (Chichester and Haymarket), *The Winter Guest* (Almeida and film), *If You're Glad, I'll be Frank, The Real Inspector Hound, The Actress and the Bishop, Gross Prophet* (Young Vic) and *Too True To Be Good* (Shared Experience). Musicals include *Sweeny Todd* (NT), *Martin Guerre* (Prince Edward) and *Into The Woods* (Donmar).

Film credits include *The Touch* (first British actress in a Bergman film), *Brazil, Sir Henry at Rawlinson's End, Five Days One Summer, American Friends* and *Mrs Caldicott's Cabbage War*.

Television credits include *Doctor Finlay, Taggart, Auf Weidersehen Pet, Dr Who, Twelfth Night, The Emigrants* and *A Christmas Carol*.

Joanne Cummins Pam

Joanne is currently in her final year at the Royal Scottish Academy.

Theatre credits at the Royal Scottish Academy of Music and Drama include *Aladdin, Tartuffe, Twelfth Night, Sunburst Finish, Electra, The Cherry Orchard, Brutopia* and *Cinderella*. Other theatre credits include *Honk!* (Hot Box Productions) and *San Diego* (The Tron).

Sharman Macdonald Writer

Sharman Macdonald's first play for The Bush was *When I Was a Girl, I Used to Scream and Shout*, which won the Evening Standard Award for Most Promising Playwright. Her other plays include *The Brave* (commissioned by the Bush Theatre), *When We Were Women*, *All Things Nice*, *Shades*, *The Winter Guest*, *Sea Urchins*, *Borders of Paradise*, *After Juliet*, Films include *Wild Flowers* and *The Winter Guest*. For Radio, *Gladly My Cross Eyed Bear*, *Sea Urchins* and *Soft Fall the Sands of Eden*. Sharman is also the author of two novels, *The Beast* and *Night Night*. For the Almeida opera season, she wrote the libretto to *Hey Persephone!*

Mike Bradwell Director

Mike trained at E15 Acting School and is Artistic Director of The Bush Theatre. He played Norman in Mike Leigh's award winning film *Bleak Moments* and was an actor/musician with *The Ken Campbell Road Show* and an underwater escapologist with Hirst's *Carivari*.

Mike founded Hull Truck Theatre Company in 1971 and directed all their shows for 10 years, including his own plays *Oh What*, *Bridget's House*, *Bed Of Roses*, *Ooh La La!*, *Still Crazy After All These Years* and new plays by Doug Lucie, Alan Williams and Peter Tinniswood. Mike has directed 35 shows at The Bush including *Hard Feelings* by Doug Lucie, *Unsuitable for Adults* by Terry Johnson, *The Fosdyke Sagas* by Bill Tidy and Alan Plater, *Love and Understanding* by Joe Penhall (also at The Long Wharf Theatre, U.S.A), *Love You, Too* by Doug Lucie, *Dead Sheep* and *Shang-a-Lang* by Catherine Johnson (also 1999 national tour), *Howie The Rookie* by Mark O'Rowe (also Civic Theatre, Tallaght and Andrew's Lane theatres, Dublin, 1999 Edinburgh Festival, Plymouth Theatre Royal, The Tron, Glasgow, PS122 New York and the Magic Theatre, San Francisco), *Dogs Barking* by Richard Zajdllic, Normal by Helen Blakeman, *Resident Alien* by Tim Fountain (also for New York Theater Workshop), *Flamingos* by Jonathan Hall, *Blackbird* by Adam Rapp, *Little Baby Nothing* by Catherine Johnson, *Airsick* by Emma Frost, *adrenalin...heart* by Georgia Fitch (also at the Tram Theatre, Tokyo), *The Glee Club* by Richard Cameron (also at The Duchess Theatre 2002 and at Bolton Octagon, Galway Arts Festival and on tour in 2004) and *Gong Donkeys* by Richard Cameron .

Mike has also directed new plays by Helen Cooper, G.F Newman, Jonathan Gems, Richard Cameron, Flann O'Brien and Terry Johnson at Hampstead Theatre, the Tricycle, King's Head, West Yorkshire Playhouse, Science Fiction Theatre of Liverpool, The National Theatre of Brent, The Rude Players of Winnipeg and The Royal Court, where he was Associate Director.

Mike has written and directed for television including *The Writing on the Wall*, *Games Without Frontiers*, *Chains of Love* and *Happy Feet* (BBC Screen One).

Robin Don Designer

Among the many productions he has designed since Sharman Macdonald's first play *When I Was a Girl I Used to Scream and Shout* are; *Stepping Out* (West Yorkshire Playhouse), *Kiss of the Spiderwoman* (The Bush), *Ticket of Leave Man* (RNT), *Les Enfants du Paradis* (Royal Shakespeare Company), *A Walk in the Woods* (Comedy Theatre), *Fool for Love* (Donmar), *Top Girls* (Citizens Theatre, Glasgow) and *The Anniversary* (The Garrick).

Musicals include *The Rocky Horror Show* (Piccadilly), *Song and Dance* (Palace), *Ziegfield* (Palladium), *Chicago* (National Theatre, Iceland) and *The Boy Friend* (Old Vic). Opera and Ballet credits include productions for Aldeburgh Festival, Lyric Opera of Chicago, Opera de Lyon, Opera North, Royal Opera House, San Francisco Opera, Sydney Opera House and Quanzhou Ballet, China.

Film credits include *The Winter Guest* (with Oscar winner Emma Thompson, directed by Alan Rickman). Robin's design for the Almeida's production of Sharman Macdonald's *The Winter Guest* received the 1996 British Theatre Managers' Award for Best Designer. In the same year the Critic's Circle named Robin Designer of the Year. For Britain he won the Golden Troika at the Prague International Theatre Design Quadrienalle.

Gerry Jenkinson Lighting Designer

Gerry started lighting bands in 1966. Since then has been lighting Citizens Theatre Productions in Glasgow and internationally. He has worked on numerous drama productions nationwide including The National Theatre, The Royal Shakespeare Company, Old Vic, Royal Court, Hampstead, Almeida, Kings Head, Donmar, Stratford East, Richmond and The Bush Theatre.

Gerry has also worked abroad in New York, Paris, Ludwigshafen, Dublin's Abbey and Gaiety.

Opera and Ballet for Covent Garden, English National, Scottish, Welsh, North, Kent, Glyndebourne, Aldeburgh, Buxton and Sadlers Wells.

Numerous West End credits include *Rocky Horror Show, Gloo Joo, Mother Courage, The Vortex, Design for Living, Heat of the Day, Torch Song Trilogy, The Mystery of the Roe Bouquet, A Madhouse in Goa, The Entertainer, The Original Phantom of the Opera, The Invisible Man, Lady Windermere's Fan, A Woman of No Importance, Travels with my Aunt, Oleanna, Rupert Street Lonely Hearts Club, Giovanni D'Arco, The Pearl Fishers* and *Semi-Monde*.

Recently Gerry has been working on *Golden Boy, Two Sisters and a Piano, True West, Barber of Seville* and *The Globe* at Hampton Court.

Tom Zwitserlood Sound Designer

Tom Zwitserlood is Head of Sound at the Royal Lyceum Theatre in Edinburgh.

Besides the sound design on the Lyceum shows he also does most of the designs for Lyceum Youth Theatre and worked on the Scottish tour last year of *The Woman who Cooked her Husband*. Before moving to Scotland Tom worked in the Netherlands as a sound technician for renowned drama company Het Zuidelijk Toneel.

Jemima Levick Assistant Director

Directing credits include *Hambledog* and *Hopping Clogs* (Hill Street Theatre and The English Theatre Warsaw), *Solemn Mass for a Full Moon in Summer* (Gateway Theatre).

Assistant Directing credits include *Othello* (Royal Lyceum), *Sweet Fanny Adams in Eden* (Stellar Quines Theatre Co.), *15 Seconds* (The Traverse Theatre). Jemima is also project coordinator for Class Act Russia (The Traverse Theatre).

Her post as Assistant Director is supported by the Scottish Arts Council Trainee Director Scheme.

At The Bush Theatre

Artistic Director	**Mike Bradwell**
Executive Producer	**Fiona Clark**
General Manager	**Brenda Newman**
Literary Manager	**Abigail Gonda**
Marketing Manager	**Gillian Jones**
Technical Manager	**Matt Kirby**
Resident Stage Manager	**Ros Terry**
Literary Assistant	**Holly Hughes**
Assistant General Manager	**Nic Wass**
Box Office Supervisor	**Dominique Gerrard**
Box Office Assistants	**Rowan Bangs**
	Amanda Wright
Front of House Duty Managers	**Kellie Batchelor**
	Adrian Christopher
	Sarah Hunter
	Lois Tucker
	Catherine Nix–Collins
	Sarah O'Neill
Associate Artists	**Tanya Burns**
	Es Devlin
Sheila Lemon Writer in Residence	**Jennifer Farmer**
Pearson Writer in Residence	**Steve Thompson**

The Bush Theatre continues to develop its Writers Development Programme with the generous support of the Peggy Ramsay Foundation Award 2002.

The Bush Theatre
Shepherds Bush Green
London W12 8QD

The Alternative Theatre Company Ltd. (The Bush Theatre)
is a Registered Charity number: 270080
Co. registration number 1221968
VAT no. 228 3168 73

The Bush Theatre

The Bush Theatre opened in April 1972 in the upstairs dining room of The Bush Hotel, Shepherds Bush Green. The room had previously served as Lionel Blair's dance studio. Since then, The Bush has become the country's leading new writing venue with over 350 productions, premiering the finest new writing talent.

"One of the most vibrant theatres in Britain, and a consistent hotbed of new writing talent." Midweek magazine

Playwrights whose works have been performed here at The Bush include:
Stephen Poliakoff, Robert Holman, Tina Brown, Snoo Wilson, John Byrne, Ron Hutchinson, Terry Johnson, Beth Henley, Kevin Elyot, Doug Lucie, Dusty Hughes, Sharman Macdonald, Billy Roche, Tony Kushner, Catherine Johnson, Philip Ridley, Richard Cameron, Jonathan Harvey, Richard Zajdlic, Naomi Wallace, David Eldridge, Conor McPherson, Joe Penhall, Helen Blakeman, Lucy Gannon, Mark O'Rowe and Charlotte Jones.

The theatre has also attracted major acting and directing talents including Bob Hoskins, Alan Rickman, Antony Sher, Stephen Rea, Frances Barber, Lindsay Duncan, Brian Cox, Kate Beckinsale, Patricia Hodge, Simon Callow, Alison Steadman, Jim Broadbent, Tim Roth, Jane Horrocks, Gwen Taylor, Mike Leigh, Mike Figgis, Mike Newell and Richard Wilson.

Victoria Wood and Julie Walters first worked together at The Bush, and Victoria wrote her first sketch on an old typewriter she found backstage.

In over 30 years, The Bush has won over one hundred awards and recently received The Peggy Ramsay Foundation Project Award 2002. Bush plays, including most recently The Glee Club, have transferred to the West End. Off-Broadway transfers include Howie the Rookie and Resident Alien. Film adaptations include Beautiful Thing and Disco Pigs. Bush productions have toured throughout Britain, Europe North America and Asia, most recently Stitching, Adrenalin... Heart (representing the UK in the Tokyo International Arts Festival, 2004) and The Glee Club (UK National Tour, Autumn 2004).

Every year we receive over fifteen hundred scripts through the post, and we read them all. According to The Sunday Times:

"What happens at The Bush today is at the very heart of tomorrow's theatre"

That's why we read all the scripts we receive and will continue to do so.

Mike Bradwell
Artistic Director

Fiona Clark
Executive Producer

Be There At The Beginning

The Bush Theatre is a writer's theatre – dedicated to commissioning, developing and producing exclusively new plays. Up to seven writers each year are commissioned and we offer a bespoke programme of workshops and one-to-one dramaturgy to develop their plays. Our international reputation of over thirty years is built on consistently producing the very best work to the very highest standard.

With your help this work can continue to flourish.

The Bush Theatre's Patron Scheme delivers an exciting range of opportunities for individual and corporate giving, offering a closer relationship with the theatre and a wide range of benefits from ticket offers to special events. Above all, it is an ideal way to acknowledge your support for one of the world's greatest new writing theatres.

To join, please pick up an information pack from the foyer, call 020 7602 3703 or email info@bushtheatre.co.uk

We would like to thank our current members and invite you to join them!

Rookies
Anonymous
Anonymous
Anonymous
David Brooks
Geraldine Caulfield
Sian Hansen
Lucy Heller
Mr G Hopkinson
Ray Miles
Malcolm & Liliane Ogden
Clare Rich & Robert Marshall
Martin Shenfield

Beautiful Things
Anonymous
Alan Brodie
Kate Brooke
Clive Butler
Clyde Cooper
Patrick and Anne Foster
Vivien Goodwin
Sheila Hancock
David Hare
William Keeling
Laurie Marsh
Mr & Mrs A Radcliffe
John Reynolds
Mr and Mrs George Robinson
Tracey Scoffield
Barry Serjent
Brian D Smith

Glee Club
Anonymous
The Hon Mrs Giancarla
Alen-Buckley
Jim Broadbent
Nick Marston

Lone Star
Silver Star

Bronze Corporate Membership
Act Productions Ltd
Anonymous

Silver Corporate Membership
The Agency
Oberon Books Ltd
PFD

Platinum Corporate Membership
Anonymous

ROYAL
LYCEUM
THEATRE
COMPANY

The Royal Lyceum Theatre Company is Edinburgh's premier producing large scale theatre company. With an international reputation for an annual programme of work that is exciting, inspirational and highly relevant to contemporary audiences, the Company currently produces a subscription season of six plays from September to May each year, and a children's show at Christmas. In May the theatre is leased to the Scottish International Children's Festival and in August to the Edinburgh International Festival. In addition, youth theatre workshops take place in summer culminating in performances on the main stage and the work of visiting companies is occasionally presented to complement the Company's own programme.

The Company is just about to mark its fortieth anniversary. It has celebrated the best of Scottish and UK talent throughout its existence under the artistic leadership of Kenny Ireland, Clive Perry, Sir Richard Eyre, Tom Fleming and Bill Bryden, to name but a few. Mark Thomson, the current Artistic Director, was appointed in April 2003.

Recent successes have included an acclaimed production of *Uncle Varick* adapted from Chekhov's *Uncle Vanya* by John Byrne and starring Brian Cox; Des Dillon's award-winning new play *Six Black Candles*; and a highly lauded production of John Osborne's *Look Back in Anger* with David Tennent and Kelly Reilly produced in assocation with Theatre Royal Bath Productions.

The Royal Lyceum Theatre Company was founded in 1965 and the company is based in the Royal Lyceum Theatre, a magnificent example of late Victorian theatre architecture with its stage set behind a proscenium arch. The theatre was built for theatrical entrepreneurs Howard and Wyndham by CJ Phipps and was opened in September 1883.

General information

Board of directors
Donald Emslie (Chair), Richard Findlay (Vice Chair), David Anderson, Jennifer Black, Cllr Steve Cardownie, Cllr Ricky Henderson, Richard Keith, Vikram Lall, Cllr John Longstaff, Cllr Elizabeth Maginnis, Neil Menzies, Cllr Eric Milligan.

Registered office
Royal Lyceum Theatre Company, 30B Grindlay Street, Edinburgh EH3 9AX.
Registered in Scotland No. 62065. Legal advisors: Tods Murray LLP.
The Royal Lyceum is a registered charity SC010509.

Administration
Tel: 0131 248 4800
Email: info@lyceum.org.uk

Fax: 0131 228 3955
Web: www.lyceum.org.uk

Royal Lyceum Theatre Company staff

Mark Thomson	Artistic Director
Linda Crooks	Administrative Producer
David Butterworth	Head of Production

PRODUCTION

Caitlin Blair	Wardrobe Assistant / Maker
Tommy Brophy	Chief Stage Technician
Kelly Butterfield	Assistant Stage Manager
Fiona Clark	Head Scenic Artist
Ruth Crighton	Company Stage Manager
Jenny Cruikshank	Costume Hire
Jason Dailly	Workshop Manager
Carolyn Davis	Wardrobe Supervisor
George Ewing	Stage Technician
Maggie Kennedy	Costume Hire
Trish Kenny	Wardrobe Maintenance & Dresser
Kevin Leary	Deputy Scenic Artist
Claire Loughran	Costume Hire
Ross MacFarlane	Deputy Electrician
Sarah Marshall	Deputy Carpenter
Hamish Millar	Stage Technician / Flyman
Andy Murray	Chief Electrician
Richard O'Connor	Master Carpenter
Adi Powers	Assistant Electrician
Clifford Simms	Storesman / Driver
Isobel Skea	Wardrobe Assistant / Maker
Karen Sorley	Deputy Wardrobe Supervisor & Cutter
Dan Travis	Deputy Stage Manager
Claire Williamson	Assistant Stage Manager
Heather Wilson	Deputy Stage Manager
Tom Zwitserlood	Head of Sound

ADMINISTRATION

Fiona Semple	Accountant
Vaila Hughson	Assistant Accountant
Ruth Butterworth	Administration Manager
Rosie Kellagher	Administration Assistant

BUSINESS LIAISON & SPONSORSHIP

Katie Bowling	Business Development Manager (0131 248 4827)

EDUCATION

Lucy Vaughan	Head of Education
Colin Bradie	LYT Leader
Alison Reeves	Education Officer

FRONT OF HOUSE

Danica Gilland	Theatre Manager
Jacqui Nagib	Deputy Theatre Manager

MARKETING

Shirley Monteith	Marketing Manager
Stephen Gray	Communications Manager (0131 248 4822)
Caroline Donald	Press & Marketing Assistant

Sponsorship & Corporate Support at Royal Lyceum Theatre Company

There are many ways companies and organisations can support the work of Scotland's leading producing theatre.

Whether your interest lies in corporate entertaining, sponsorship and branding or helping the social development of our communities through outreach and access initiatives, we can provide the opportunities.

To find out how you can join our valued supporters, please contact:

Katie Bowling, Business Development Manager, Royal Lyceum Theatre Company, 30b Grindlay Street, Edinburgh, EH3 9AX.

T: 0131 248 4827   email: development@lyceum.org.uk

We thank the following organisations for their valued support this year:

Sponsors
Arts & Business Scotland
British Airways Travel Shops
ESPC (UK) Limited
Haagen Dazs
Hewlett Packard
The List
Oculus Multimedia
Royal Mail
Standard Life

Corporate Members
Adam & Company
Fairway Forklifts
NVT Computing Limited
Royal Bank of Scotland
Scottish Life
Springfords
Turcan Connell
Willis UK & Ireland Limited

hampstead theatre

Hampstead Theatre is a new writing theatre. Over the past forty years, it has established a unique reputation for the ambition, quality and success of the new plays it has produced.

Central to our programming policy is the desire to provide opportunities for new plays developed and produced outside of London to be seen in the capital, without having to meet the expectations of the West End. I am thrilled to be presenting *The Girl With Red Hair* in our programme.

As well as making a vital contribution to the national and international scene, we have always sought to reflect the concerns and aspirations of those communities living and working within reach of the theatre. Our far reaching education programme, for example, seeks to encourage people of all ages to get involved in our work as artists and audiences, and attracts over twenty thousand people annually. Our studio theatre, The Michael Frayn Space, provides a focus for this work.

Hampstead Theatre has recently enjoyed its most successful six months in its new building, with two sell-out productions: the world premiere of *Losing Louis,* which has transferred to the Trafalgar in Whitehall, and *Primo,* Antony Sher's remarkable adaptation of *If This Is A Man* by Primo Levi. Our Spring/Summer season continues with the only London dates for award-winning playwright Roy Williams' latest play, *Little Sweet Thing.* Following this, we will be presenting two bold new plays on a single theme: *Osama The Hero* by Dennis Kelly and *A Single Act* by Jane Bodie. These plays will run in repertory, performed by the same actors, with both plays enriching each other as an urgent response to today's world.

If you would like to find out more about Hampstead Theatre, join our free email list by emailing 'subscribe list' to info@hampsteadtheatre.com or by visiting our website.

Anthony Clark
Artistic Director

Tickets & information
www.hampsteadtheatre.com
020 7722 9301

Hampstead Theatre Supporters

Charity Registration No 218506.
Company Registration No 707180. VAT No 230 3818 91

Sharman Macdonald
Girl with Red Hair

faber and faber

First published in 2005
by Faber and Faber Limited
3 Queen Square London WCIN 3AU

Typeset by Country Setting, Kingsdown, Kent CT14 8ES
Printed in England by Mackays of Chatham plc, Chatham, Kent

A CIP record for this book
is available from the British Library

ISBN 0–571–22006–1

2 4 6 8 10 9 7 5 3 1

Characters

Stuart
A truck driver. Cropped bristly hair. Still slender though
he's in his middle years. Long-fingered. Even his touch
on the hot wooden table is sensual. Forty-seven years old.

Cath
The cook/manageress of the inn. Roslyn's mother. She's
a woman who doesn't live any more, she just functions.
She's not unpleasant, just contained. Forty-five years old.

Izzy
The minister's daughter. Doesn't want to grow up. Roslyn
used to babysit for her. Of course she worshipped her.
Thirteen years old.

Corinne
Never a friend of Roslyn's. Now she's going out
with her boyfriend. Seventeen years old.

Matt
Sings and plays guitar. Corinne's boyfriend.
Roslyn's ex-boyfriend. Eighteen years old.

Sadie
A woman of the town. Aching for life in spite
of her sixty-six years. Or because of them.

Ina
Her lifelong friend. Sixty-eight years old.

Pam
Izzy's friend. The same chronological age as Izzy
but years and years older in her head.

A seaside town, Fife, Scotland.

Sunshine, mellow, long-beamed. The world's steeped in warmth. The sea's lazy in the heat.

Izzy's leaning. Waiting. Watching everything: watching anything.

Stuart's sitting at a sun-bleached wooden table on the sunlit prom. He has a magazine. He isn't reading it. There's a dry tree against the white stone wall behind him, covered in fairy lights. Unlit. He leans back, eyes closed, face up to the sun.

Yacht pennants, far away, flicker in the wind; sing at the tops of masts with a tinny sound.

Cath yells from a doorway.

Cath Do you want anything?

Stuart What've you got?

She brings a menu over to the table. Stuart smiles at her.

I could do with some company.

Cath D'you see it on the menu?

She goes back to the doorway; leans there; rests for a moment; wipes her hands on her wrap-around white chef's apron; turns her face up to the sun.

Stuart Small pleasures, eh?

She doesn't answer.

Sun and sea. What more can you want, eh?

Still no answer.

Stuart watches her. His table's outside an inn on the prom. Weeds grow through the cracked paving. Scattered stones are lying there chucked up by the winter sea and left. The railings are broken and rusted. It's a ruined place, beautiful though, with its shabby remnants of an old gentility. There's a spiral staircase going down from the prom to the sea.

Stuart Nice view, eh?

It's not the sea view he's looking at. Cath knows that. She turns away, looks out at the hard glitter of the water.

Heaven, eh?

Stuart runs his hands over the rough wood of the sun-hot table.

See, when I die, if God wants me to live with him and all his angels he'll have to furnish me with a wooden table for the sun to warm.

She ignores him. He doesn't care.

See the way it opens up the grain, the heat. You want to know what beauty is.? Here's what beauty is. You come here and feel this. Come on and have a feel.

Feast for the senses, eh?

His look encompasses the menu in his hand, the world around him and her in it.

Takes a stranger to show you. The beauty you live with. It takes a stranger.

He gets out his mobile.

A string of coloured bulbs on a wire stretch between ornate lamp-posts that gave their last light long ago. The wire twangs in the wind.

Cath Can you swim?

Stuart Eh?

Cath See that rock. That's where the signal is.

He's still watching her. Lazily.

Stuart So then. I've no transport. No phone. Heaven indeed.

Cath There's a garage down the road. And a phone in the bar.

Stuart Don't spoil it.

Cath They'll fix your truck.

Stuart I can't hear you. (*His hands move over the table.*) Life gives you presents. You have to know to recognise the presents Life gives you. They don't come twice.

The sun's shining. The light's clear. The sea's gleaming.
   A bleach of bright light, so bright it almost hides the sea.
   Corinne comes out of the light. She's carrying wild flowers.

Izzy He'll pull these out, the cemetery man.

Corinne If they were weeds he would.

Izzy Roses are what he likes. Hyacinths for the spring.

Corinne Stay Well, they're called. You get white ones but I've only got the pink.

Izzy 'Stay Well'? For a grave? 'Stay Put' – that's what you really mean.

Corinne I'm just bringing her flowers.

7

Beat.

Izzy Can I come with you?

Corinne Be different if they stank.

Izzy Because a thing doesn't have a scent doesn't mean you can't smell it.

He'll have them on the compost heap, the cemetery man, soon as look at them, he will.

Corinne I get on fine with him.

Izzy 'I get on fine with him.'

Beat.

You're just filled with the sin of vanity, Corinne Maeve O'Halloran. Top to toe.

Corinne And what are you filled with?

Izzy The devil'll get you and he'll take you down to Hell and he'll sit you in front of a mirror for all eternity. And it'll be the devil's own mirror. And it won't be your pretty face that you're so fond of that you see therein.

Corinne Do you never get tired of it, eh? The sound of your own voice, Izzy? On and on it goes.

Izzy All you'll see is your own black soul. And it won't be pleasant.

Corinne On and on and on.

Izzy And there's no feminine wiles that you possess that'll set you free of the devil's own mirror, not once he's sat you down on his dressing-table stool.

Corinne That's your daddy talking.

Izzy I don't need my father to tell me the devil's mind.

Corinne He'll get apoplexy and die in his pulpit, the lather he works himself up into.

Izzy And the jaws of Hell will open up at his feet and with his dying breath he'll cry out to the assembled congregation, 'I told you so.' And the flames will devour him.

Beat.

Corinne Jesus, it's so fucking hot.

Izzy I get dilatory in the heat. Lackadaisical, that's what I get.

A gleam of light.
Izzy waves up at Cath. Cath doesn't wave.

My mum says she's lost a friend. To another world she's lost her. My mum's waiting. She says the real Cath'll come back one day, from the other world. Something'll bring her back. My dad says my mum's over-sanguine. That woman's gone for ever. Where no one can follow her, that's where she's gone to. My dad says.

Corinne You take a risk when you have children.

Izzy I'm never going to have them.

Corinne You'll be empty, then.

They watch Cath turn away.

In the café.

Stuart Know what I want? Do you?

Looking at Cath. Smiling.
She has to turn back, Cath.

Have you a room for the night?

Cath Several.

Stuart I like a big room.

There are two spires looming over the prom, and a graveyard.
    Cath turns to go back inside.
    Lace edges below her skirt.

Stuart Your slip's showing.

She turns and looks at him for a moment. Doesn't smile, doesn't frown, just looks at him. He looks back.

Shelf-paper, my dad used to call it. 'Perfume and pearls, son,' he'd say to me. 'That's what the angels'll wear when I get to Heaven. Perfume, pearls and a satin slip. And if they don't I'll hand God in my notice and go right on down to the other place.'

Cath Pearls are for tears.

Stuart No tears in Heaven.

Cath leaves him. He stretches in the heat.
    Matt goes down the metal stairway to the beach. His guitar's slung over his shoulder. He's carrying a bag of food. Bright light. Like the sun sparking up off metal. Waves rush and pull at the stones on the shore. The wind blows. Cath watches him.

Cath (*calling sharply*) You're not lighting a fire are you?

Matt What if I am?

Cath Are you cooking?

Matt I'll keep the smoke away from you.

Cath Can you order the heavens now? Amongst your other talents.

Matt I'll fan it away from you.

Cath See you do.

Cath lets the door swing to behind her. Matt hunkers down on the beach, still for a moment like a cuffed child.

Flashes of sun through the branches. Rippling shadows of leaves. Green shade. The cemetery.

A grave covered in flowers and glass jars. Some with candles in them. Some with notes, sealed in plastic to keep the rain out.

Corinne's lighting the candles.

Izzy 'Here,' she said, Roslyn. On my birthday, this was. And she gave me this. (*She slips a silver bracelet round and round her wrist.*) 'The silver link,' she said. 'So anywhere you are, you touch that and it'll be like we're touching. Like our minds are touching.' From the time she was wee Roslyn had a silver bracelet. From the time she was born. Her mother keeps her baby one in a box. It's gone all black now, the silver. They had to cut it off her baby wrist. Her mother left it so long that the baby fat just engulfed it and they couldn't get it over her chubby wee hand. 'Fatty, fatty, fatty,' my Aunt Cath said she was, 'but awful bonny.' Everyone that means something to her . . .

Corinne Meant.

Izzy . . . we've all got silver bracelets. The ones she liked. Course she didn't know you. Her mother keeps her baby teeth in a china box from Limoges with '*dents de lait*' in gold on its roof. So that's what she's got left of her daughter. And the stitch that they took out when they sewed up her chin when she fell off the wall at primary school, that's in the box too.

Stuart takes off his shirt. Picks up his magazine. Puts it down. Rubs the sweat from his belly. Rubs the sweat from his shaved head and stubbly chin. Loves the sunshine.

Izzy You can talk to her if you want.

Corinne How d'you mean?

Izzy Talk to Roslyn.

Corinne It's not like she's here, is it, to talk to?

Izzy All the letters, see. What are they here for? What do folk leave them for if she isn't here?

Beat.

Well, I don't need to write letters for the rain to get. I can talk to her. And she listens and she talks back. And I'm saying you can too. I'll help you if you want. I mean you must have a lot you want to talk to her about.

Corinne If I was dead and my spirit was free to roam, I wouldn't hang around here.

Izzy She likes it. And I do. There's no dog shite. He's very particular about the dogs, the cemetery man. So you can wear your bare feet. You can walk in your bare feet in perfect confidence.
You've a lot in common after all, the two of you.

Corinne's looking at Matt on the beach. He's laying a fire. Making a circle of stones. Building up driftwood.

Corinne He hasn't enough wood.

Izzy A common interest.

Corinne Let him make his fire.

There's a languor about the way she's watching Matt that makes Izzy look away.

I've a dress at home I bought. Later I'll meet him. When I've changed I will.

Izzy Don't you want to talk to her?

Beat.

She'd've run down to him. Soon as she saw him she would.

Corinne There's an art to a beach fire.

Izzy The things she knows about him. The things she could tell you. (*She hooks a letter out of a jar. Reads it.*) 'Ros, are you there? Roslyn?' Bet you don't know who this is from.

Corinne Bet I do.

Izzy 'I miss talking to you.' Bet you didn't know he'd written that.

Corinne closes her eyes, quotes the letter.

Corinne 'I miss everything about you. The smell of your skin. The chance I might meet you on a street corner when I'm not expecting to see you. Lying on the beach, I miss, when the stones are still hot from the sunshine though the dark's coming in, and you beside me. Lying there quiet the two of us because we don't need to talk, because we've got tomorrow to talk in. I miss knowing there's tomorrow. I miss running with you. Laughing with you. I miss the touch of your hair that had the red sun in it. Your hair like silk on my fingers.'

Izzy touches Corinne's hair. Lets it run through her fingers.

Corinne Don't.

Izzy This is how he did it. How he did it to Roslyn. The way I'm doing it now.

13

Corinne Stop it.

Izzy Don't you want to know?

Corinne No.

Izzy In the garden I used to see him. On the beach.

Corinne Other people watch MTV.

Corinne grabs Izzy's hand.

Izzy (*hurting*) I've always liked the outdoors.

Corinne lets go.
Izzy's twisting her bracelet round and round her wrist.
Stuart makes a hat of his magazine and puts it on his head.
Matt's bracelet gets caught in the sacking of the food bag. He untangles it.

Izzy There's no letters from me here. You won't find any. I can talk to her like she's still alive. Easy as anything, I can. I don't even have to be in the cemetery.

The sun shines bright.
Matt lights the fire. Waits for it to catch. Rolls potatoes up in silver foil.
Corinne can just see him. Just hear the crackle of the dry seaweed and the driftwood.

'Don't touch her hand,' they said, when she lay beneath the sheet. The mortuary people. They'd washed the blood out of her hair, my dad said. My dad christened her. Buried her grandmother. Married her parents. Her hand was hurt. They didn't want her mother to touch it, standing there to identify her. Of course, though, her mother rushed forward, wanted to take her hand out from under the cover, to hold it. Wanted to hold her daughter. It was my dad that held her back. He has a very sad job, my dad, which explains some of the things about him. See, he only believes in Hell. That's the cosmology I live with. My dad's not sure about Heaven but he knows there's a Hell. So I know there's a Hell too. And there's a devil but there is no God. I don't know how we cling to life at all, me and my dad. She felt nothing in the crash. She was asleep. She didn't see her life go. If she'd known it was going she would have held on to it. Her face was unmarked. Her mother stroked her hair. They had the same hair. They were friends, her mother and her. Her mother misses her as a friend and a sister. She almost doesn't miss her as a daughter at all. For months she came to the graveside every day. Then her husband left her and she was alone. 'Who can blame him?' my dad said. She'd lost her daughter, Cath, but her husband, he'd lost them both, his daughter and his wife as well; for though Cath wasn't dead, she might as well've been.

Matt plays a light riff on the guitar. Light gleams off the frets.

Matt takes off his T-shirt. Wipes off the sweat with it. Izzy watches him.

Corinne You've got a crush on him, haven't you?

Izzy You'll have to be dead to get letters like he writes her.

Corinne It'll pass, you know.

Izzy Like puppy fat?

Corinne I had a crush on my swimming teacher when I was your age.

Izzy Don't call me young.

Corinne You wait, one day you'll find someone and he'll be your very own.

Izzy 'I miss everything about you.' That's the way Matt loved Roslyn. That's the way he loves her yet. He'll never love you like that.

Wires rattle. The prom lights sway in the breeze. Shadows.

Izzy See that shadow. That's Roslyn. She's touching his skin. She's laying her cheek against it. Where the scar is where he trailed over a barbed-wire fence long, long ago. And all the flowers in the world. All the flowers you bring her won't make her let him go.

Shouting in the distance. Children's voices. Corinne turns.

Corinne Listen.

Izzy She's glad Matt's near. While he's near she thinks she hasn't died. She's kissing his shoulder where the scar is. Where the sun's made it hot. She knows how to kiss him. No one better.

Corinne I'm not forcing him to go out with me. (*She's shivering.*)

Izzy Goose walk over your grave?

The light dips. Shade.

Matt puts his T-shirt back on. Stuart shouts down from on high.

Stuart Cold?

Matt Cloud over the sun.

Stuart You'll get the haar coming in.

Matt Maybe later.

Stuart Nothing like a beach fire. Nice guitar.

Matt D'you play?

Stuart Give us.

> *Matt passes the guitar.*
> *Flickering shadow. Chords on the guitar. Leadbelly's 'Black Girl'. Matt stands looking out to sea.*
> *The shadows dance. The guitar plays.*

Corinne Jesus.

Izzy She likes the guitar. And I do. We like it better when Matt plays, Roslyn and me.

> *Izzy walks away, sits in a patch of sunlight. Twists her bracelet.*
> *The noise of a car attracts Stuart's attention. The guitar stutters to a stop.*

Stuart (*yelling*) For fuck sake. Get your left hand down. Your left hand. Dear God, woman, straighten her up. Left. Left.

> *The car door slams. The sound of capable shoes on pebbles. Ina walks towards him.*

Are you leaving it like that?

> *She draws him off a look. Says nothing. Walks on.*

Give me the keys, I'll park it straight for you.

> *She's gone.*
> *Stuart shouts to Matt. Passes the guitar back.*

Stuart Did you see that? Did you see it?

Matt You frightened her.

Stuart I'd do more than that. I'd stop them driving. Both ends of the scale. Stop them driving. Stop the young. Stop the old. I spend my life on the road. You take what I see.

Green and dappled light. Sadie sees Izzy. Sits down by her.

Sadie Does your mother know you're here?

Izzy 'Does your mother know you're here?'

Sadie I beg your pardon?

Izzy Joke.

Sadie Of course, when you're young you crack them, jokes. You have no choice. In your middle years you find the strength to give them up. They have nothing to do with wit, jokes. You find that out when you're old, being the butt of them.

Izzy You looked like a ghost coming up on me.

Sadie Aren't there bad people enough in this world without adding ghosts to them?

Izzy My mother says life's for living and I don't have to be in till dark.

Sadie It won't be dark till midnight.

Izzy What could happen to me? Who're you looking for?

Sadie We were more free in my young day. There were no bad people then. And no ghosts, for no one died then. We wandered the world and the days were long. I went for rides with Cranston Ray. See his hydrangea.

Izzy Awful dry flowers, hydrangeas.

Sadie He had a motorbike then. He knew all the secret bays, Cranston Ray.

Izzy I've my friend buried here.

Sadie We've all got friends buried here. That's where my social life is, six feet deep.

*They're both looking at Corinne planting the wild
flowers in the sunshine.*

Poor Roslyn. Poor wee girl. My God, I was still closeted
at seventeen. I suffered from a mother that was overfond.
There she lies, my mother, over there with the chrysanths.
They can be stiff, chrysanths. No give in them.
   What's her name?

Izzy Corinne Maeve O'Halloran.

Sadie Is that not Catholic? Ask her to tend my grave
when I go. Catholics know about graves. Look at the
Spanish. You ask her.

Izzy She'll just plant weeds in it.

   Matt strums the guitar.

Sadie Mind, I'm not done yet, not by a long chalk. I've
things I want to do yet. Just because you're old you don't
stop wanting. I want. I want the moon from out of the
sky. I want it in my hands to play with before I go to my
grave.

Izzy What's that yellow on your cheek?

Sadie Where is she?

   Izzy touches her cheek.

Izzy Yellow stuff.

Sadie It's not like her to be late.

Izzy I could get it off for you.

Sadie Is it pollen?

   *She reaches into her bag for a handkerchief. Spits on
   it. Hands it to Izzy.*

Izzy She'll get sunburnt wearing that.

Izzy rubs at Sadie's cheek.

She should preserve the pallor of her skin.

Sadie Don't rub so hard.

Izzy You want me to get it off, don't you. Spit again.

Sadie I'm glad I did my living when I did.

Izzy It's stubborn this. She won't look so attractive when she's pink.

Sadie You try to get the world to stay the same. Just while you walk through it. You try with all your might and main. And what happens? What happens. Eh? They tell you the sun is dangerous and pork crackling can kill a man.
  Feel that sun. And the wind in your hair. Feel it.

Ina slides out from behind a gravestone. Izzy screams.
Corinne turns and smiles.

Ina Where were you for God's sake?

Sadie Where were you?

Ina I met a rude man, Sadie. Such a rude man.

Izzy You frightened me.

Ina I'm sorry.

Izzy That's just a word, my dad says. And it cuts no ice.

Ina I know you.

She's out of breath, Ina. She sits.

Izzy Don't sit there.

Ina I taught your mother. She was a cheeky girl.
  Is that valerian she's planting?

Sadie sits beside her.

Sadie This stone's hot.

Izzy You shouldn't sit on gravestones.

Ina They should be cold, gravestones, that's their proper nature.

Izzy They all have tongues down there. They have tongues to speak with and ears to listen and you're sitting on them. (*Izzy backs away.*)

Ina What do you bother your head for? What do you bother talking to them for? The young.

Izzy Wait till you're in your boxes, the both of you. Wait till people sit on your heads. Then you'll see.

Ina We're aliens to them.

Izzy runs down onto the prom. Corinne calls after her.

Corinne Izzy? Izzy!

Matt looks round from his fire. His sausages splutter. He turns back to them. Pokes them with a stick. He takes four bananas out of the food bag. Splits them open with a knife. Puts cinnamon in the split, sugar and chocolate vermicelli. Wraps them in tinfoil.
   Pam stands on the flat roof outside her bedroom, watches Izzy climb down onto the beach. Pam's arms are full of Lucozade and peanut butter, cigarettes and matches. Her bedroom window's open behind her. The muslin curtains blow.
   Stuart stands and leans on the table watches Izzy climb down onto the prom. Goes to the kitchen door.

Stuart Are you one of those microwave cooks?

Cath They have their place.

Stuart In this kitchen?

Cath Sometimes. Do you have a problem with that?

Stuart I like my food fresh-cooked.

Cath I make a good fish soup.

Stuart Bouillabaisse?

Cath Fish soup.

Stuart Go on then.

Cath Salad?

Stuart That thing with the raspberries.

   Beat.

Do you have a name I can call you?

Cath Cath.

Stuart (*sings*)
   Oh I will take you home, Cathleen
   To where your heart is free from pain.

Cath Cath'll do.

   Stuart goes on singing.

*Pam lays the food down on the flat felt roof half-covered
in creeper. She opens the jar of peanut butter sticks a
knife in, gets out a good dollop of peanut butter, eats it
off the knife. Washes it down with a swig of Lucozade.
Takes a cigarette out of the packet, lights up. Checks no
one's watching her through the bedroom window. Looks
out from the roof along the prom. She's looking for Izzy.
Can't see her. Lies down on the warm roof, takes a long
drag of the cigarette. Blows smoke into the summer air.
Stretches her hand along the hot roof-felt. Sits up, looks
out along the prom again.*

The sun shines bright. The shadows clear. Sadie's fiddling in her bag.

Ina Give me your hat, Sadie. Give it to me.

   Sadie's hat's battered. Ina dunts it against her leg.

Sadie Died long ago, that hat.

Ina A steaming's what that needs.

Sadie Long, long ago.

Ina A good steaming.

Sadie It was always a disappointment, that hat.

Ina You were supposed to meet me in the Flamingo tea shop at half past three. There.

   She fits the hat on Sadie's head.

Sadie I was not.

Ina The Pink Flamingo.

Sadie Here, I was meeting you.

Ina I nearly got the police, Sadie.

Sadie Here, we said. I waited.

Ina I wrote it down. (*She takes out her diary.*)

Sadie Where's the one I gave you?

Ina See. See here.

Sadie I don't deny you wrote it down.

Ina The Pink Flamingo.

Sadie It was black the one I gave you.

Ina What's that yellow on your cheek?

*The breeze blows, the shadows shift. Sadie rubs at her
cheek. Moves away.*

Sadie If you fall asleep under a yew tree, you wake up
dead.

Ina Looks like nicotine.

Sadie I don't want to sit under a yew tree.

Their voices are raised. Corinne looks across at them.

Ina Keeping a person waiting. Keeping a friend waiting.
Worrying a person.

Sadie I would have changed it. If you'd said. If you'd
said you didn't like it I would have changed it for you.

Ina What's wrong with you?

Sadie If we were meeting at the Pink Flamingo. If that's
the arrangement we made. The Pink Flamingo. What are
you doing here, Ina? That's what I don't understand.
How did you know you'd find me here? Ina? Answer me
that.

Ina sees Corinne staring at them.

Ina Did you see the lilies?

Sadie They've a heady scent.

Ina Who leaves them, Sadie? On his grave, lilies.

Sadie There's a wonderful opulence to a lily.

Ina I carried roses on my wedding day. I only ever bring
him roses.

Sadie Nothing wrong with a rose. As long as they're not
yellow. There's no scent to a yellow rose.

Ina I wouldn't carry lilies. Not though he asked me. 'I'll
have roses,' says I. 'You can keep your lilies. I'll not have
them trailing their pollen down my dress.' Like ear wax.

24

Izzy's watching Matt cook the sausages.

Matt What?

Izzy Nothing.

Matt Hungry?

Izzy How come they're not bursting?

Matt Secret.
 What?

Izzy You shouldn't smoke.

Matt They're from the health-food shop.

Izzy That makes it so much better.

Ina You're awful prominent alone in a tea shop. People think you've got no one.

Sadie Do you want a fruit pastille

She takes a packet of fruit pastilles out of her bag. And a letter. Lays the letter down beside her.

Ina I didn't even have a book. You're never alone with a book. Have you an orange one?

Ina takes the packet of pastilles, opens them up down the side. Sadie's fingers drum on the letter.

I've had a book for my chaperone all through the years.
 All the pastilles are exposed.
 My mother taught me that.

Sadie If she taught you nothing else.

Sadie picks up the letter. Runs her fingers over the folds in the envelope. Presses them till they're knife-sharp.

Ina Meaning?

Sadie Your mother? May she rest in death for she never did in life.

Ina Have they stopped making orange ones?

Ina watches Sadie fiddle with the letter.

Sadie See that. See where the brick is? There's a man building that himself. He's here often in the evening. Nice big man. Ex-SAS. Gentle. Of course he's lonely. He brought that boot all the way from Devon to put by the grave. And the dog lying there. She always liked dogs, his wife. And Devon.

Ina How much time do you spend here?

Sadie I've a letter, Ina.

Ina Time must hang awful heavy on your hands that you have to come here. I'm the one with the plot and the husband resting in it. Have you nothing better to do than come here?

Sadie I've a letter.

Ina Once a week I come.

Sadie It's a while I've had it.

Ina We all get letters.

Sadie Will you read it?

Ina I've letters of my own to read.

Sadie Here.

Ina Plenty letters.

Sadie Keep still, you're making this wobble.

Ina I need a wee.

Sadie Cross your legs why don't you? Are you not going to read it?

Ina Give it to me then.

Sadie What if you had your whole life and you never did anything with it? It drifted and you drifted till it drifted away.
  Ina?

Ina Do you want me to read this?

Izzy's still standing watching Matt.

Matt Got nothing better to do?

Izzy Yes.

Matt Well?

Izzy This beach belongs to everyone.

Matt Right.

Izzy I can stand here if I want.

Matt So you can.

Izzy You better not put the bananas in till the potatoes are done.

Matt Thank you.

Izzy I know where you got that scar.
  And the bracelet, I know where you got that too.

Sadie What do you think, Ina?

Ina Give me a moment.

Sadie What do you think?

Ina I need a moment, Sadie. I need a moment to take it in.

Matt's leaving the beach, climbing up to the graveyard. Izzy's watching him.
  Cath's setting the table. White damask cloth. Clips to stop it from blowing away.

Cath I've the wine list here.

Stuart What would you choose?

  Cath shrugs.

Have you been practising that?

  Cath stares at him.
    He shrugs in imitation of her.

I met this Frenchwoman once. She was forty-five years old and she was smiling. 'These are my play years,' she said. She had this shrug. You know? Like you.

Cath Must be nice to be well travelled.

Stuart 'I've loved my husband. Loved my children. Done my duty,' she said. 'These years are now for me. These years are mine.'

Cath I like a wine that states its intentions.

Stuart Do you ever smile?

Cath I'd not choose anything subtle.

Stuart Will you join me in a glass?

  Beat.

Share some wine with me, please.

Corinne puts her arms round Matt. Kisses him. He disengages.

Matt Come down to the beach.

Corinne Frightened she'll see us if we stay here?

Matt The sausages'll spoil.

Corinne I'm not changed.

Matt You look fine as you are.

Corinne I want it to be special.

Matt It's just sausages.

Corinne We can make it special. (*She picks a candle up from the grave.*) We could have candles and everything.

Matt Put that back. Put it back.

She puts the candle down.

Corinne The balls of my feet are sore from walking on tiptoe round you.

Matt Corinne . . .

Corinne I wait for you, you know. When you're not with me I wait. And when you're with me, for fuck sake, Matt, I'm still waiting.

Matt Why do you have to keep coming here?

Corinne You do.

Matt She was cleverer than me.

Corinne Was she?

Matt We grew up together. She'd do the deciding. You know? Do we sleep in the tree-house? Is the wind too high? Will we go inside? Come on, we'll go to the quarry.

Come on, we'll get the boat out. We've always been together her and me. We were always going to be together.

Corinne She liked her own way.

Matt It's how it was, that's all.

Corinne walks away down onto the beach. Matt resets the candle she disturbed. Follows slowly.

Sadie's watching Ina, still holding the letter.

Sadie Have you assimilated the information?

Ina Two weeks ago, it's dated.

Sadie That's when I got it.

Ina I see.

Sadie I wanted to show you before.

Ina Did you?

Sadie I had to know what I thought first.

Ina Fourteen days?

Sadie It's a lot to absorb.

Ina You're a gie slow thinker.

Sadie A house, Ina.

Ina An establishment, as I understand it.

Sadie The sun's shifted.

Ina My God, Sadie. It's a business for godsake.
You'll sell it of course.
Where are you going?

Sadie The sun's leaving this place.

Ina Wait a minute.

Sadie I'll buy you fish and chips.

Ina Don't go by the rocks.

Sadie Come on, Ina.

Ina Go the top way.

Sadie I thought you wanted a wee.

Ina I'm not going to the public conveniences.

Sadie Go in the chip shop, Ina. It'll not kill them to let you use their toilet.

Ina I'm not asking.

Sadie I'll ask for you.

Ina It's not within a hundred miles, this establishment of yours. It's not within two hundred.

Sadie Six hundred miles.

Ina How do you know?

Sadie I measured with a ruler.

Ina Eh?

Sadie On the map.
I went down there.

Ina You've seen it?

Sadie I went to the funeral. Of course you can't get the whole way by train.

Ina You told me you had a cold.

Sadie Of course it could do with a facelift.

Ina We could all do with that.

Sadie Ina, it's a fine property.

Ina Was it a relative?

Sadie It's a fine establishment. (*She can't meet Ina's look.*)

Ina Did you love him? The man that left you this. Sadie?

Sadie Did I say it was a man?

Ina I'm not a fool.

Matt catches hold of Corinne. Turns her round. She lets him. He touches her cheek. She kisses his hand.

Matt Look at you.

> *Matt touches Corinne's hair. Lets it run through his fingers. Exactly as Izzy showed her he did with Roslyn.*
> *Corinne catches hold of his hand.*

Corinne See where you've got her, Matt? Roslyn? Eh? Know where she is?

Matt What the fuck's wrong with you?

Corinne Right now where she is. Right there where she always is, Matt. Eh? Wound tight round your fucking neck. (*She walks away.*)

Matt Where are you going?

Corinne See me. I'm the soul of tact me. You've a beautiful friendship, Matt. Where am I going? I'm leaving you alone with your friend. Why don't you take your sausages back there. You can have a picnic on the fucking grave.

The kitchen door swings open.

Cath (*calling*) You watch that smoke, Matt.

Matt For fuck sake.

Cath I'll not tell you again.

Matt Can we not just talk to each other?

Cath The smoke.

The door swings shut.

Stuart None of my business, eh?

Matt What?

Stuart What the fuck you did to her.

Matt I did nothing.

Stuart She doesn't seem an unreasonable woman to me.

Matt I did fucking nothing.

Stuart Have it your own way.

Sadie and Ina walking.

Sadie You look at that sky. You'd think it was still day from that sky.

Ina Was it a man left it to you?

Sadie You've bad-tempered feet, do you know that, Ina? Listen to them tapping. Tap-tap-tapping away.

Ina I said was it a man?

Sadie Not the way you think.

Ina What man?

Sadie You don't know everything about me.

Ina How do I not?

Sadie Come here. Come and you listen to me. I've a proposition for you.

Ina Did you love him?

Beat.

Don't be coy, Sadie. You're too old to be coy.

Sadie Do you want to hear my proposition?

Ina Men have propositions, Sadie. That's who do the propositioning.

Fish soup. Aioli. Cheese. Scone bread. A salad. All carried in on a big wooden tray.

Stuart That's a proper tray. That's the kind of tray that speaks of a warm heart. You'd take breakfast to the one you loved on a tray like that. You'd take them breakfast in bed.
    Here. (*He tries to take it from her.*)

Cath You're the customer, I'm the proprietor.

Stuart Suit yourself.

He watches her. The dishes are square. Black and white. Carefully chosen. She sets them out round him.

It can't pay you.

Cath Up till a year ago we were busy.

Stuart I'm not complaining.

Cath You wouldn't have got a table.

Stuart I like the attention.

Beat.

You make this too?

Cath Scone bread, that's all.

Stuart Did you smile when you made it?

Cath If you don't like what's in front of you, there's a chippie up the road.

Stuart You can't put sadness into your food.

Cath You don't have to eat it.

Cath lifts the tureen to take it away.

Stuart I never said I didn't want it. (*He takes off the lid.*) You've saffron in this. There's some use tomato.

Cath A tomato soup's a tomato soup.

Stuart Is that lemon thyme?

Cath What's your name? Egon Ronay is it?

Stuart Marseilles, that's the place for bouillabaisse.

Cath Bord el kiffen.

Stuart North Africa?

Cath Outside Algiers.

Stuart You been there?

Beat.

That's what it is.

Cath This is fish soup.

Stuart You can always tell a woman that's seen the desert. You see it in her eyes.

Beat.

Strictly speaking it's a bourride you serve the aioli with.

Cath Like I said.

Stuart Eh?

Cath There's a chippie along the prom. There's raspberries under the leaves, just turned in a syrup I made with port. And pine nuts. They're fresh picked, the raspberries. Everything's fresh.

Stuart There's a woman I know, she had this big lobster. Great big thing it was. Claws? Didn't have a pot big enough to cook it in. She boiled the water. Put its backside in, cooked its back end. Should've heard it scream. Then she put its head in, cooked that. Near put me off lobster for life.

Cath Didn't put you off the woman?

Stuart I was married to her.

Beat.

Was. (*He tastes the soup.*)

Good.

Cath Is that all?

He takes a spoonful of aioli, stirs it into the soup. Tastes again. Smiles.
The sea has a Mediterranean sound that even northern seas can acquire, lush after a hot day.
Corinne flits across and across in front of a mirror in a light, short dress.

36

Pam's on a flat roof above the garden. She has Rizlas and tobacco. She's trying to roll a cigarette. Her bedroom window's open behind her. It's a double roof, the next-door bedroom window's closed.

Pam lights up. The window behind her opens. The curtains blow out. The noise startles Pam. She screams. Izzy laughs and sticks her head out of the window.

Pam Are you mental? Do you want my mum to find us?

Izzy Keep your hair on.

Pam You're late.

Izzy climbs out of the window.

Izzy You're dead white, you.

Pam I wondered where you were.

Izzy Sorry.

Pam There's phones. You could phone a person. I mean waiting. You think things when you're waiting. What are phones for but to stop people thinking things?

Izzy What the fuck's that?

Pam It's not a fucking Tampax.

Izzy Don't do that.

Pam I smoke in the game. And you do.

Izzy That's different.

Pam How the fuck is it different?

Izzy It's not you smoking, is it?

Pam It's still my lips, it's still my lungs.

Izzy It's the game though.

Down in the garden. Cath pours wine into a glass.

Stuart Join me.

   Beat.

Use the water glass. Please.

   She pours.

Cath Thank you.

Stuart I bet you have a nice smile.

Pam's smoking. Izzy's kneeling there. The creeper and the curtains blow.

Izzy Play.

Pam I didn't think you were going to come.

Izzy I'm here now, amn't I? Come on and play.

   Pam eases into the game.

Pam Roslyn's looking at herself in the mirror and it's her forehead she's looking at.

Izzy Put the cigarette out. Go on, Pam.

   Beat.
   Pam stubs the cigarette out.

Pam She says, Roslyn says, 'My ring of fire's back.' Which means she's had sex, because the hormones rage when she's had sex. And she gets spots.

Izzy 'My ring of fire's back.'

Pam You didn't touch your forehead.

Izzy I know how she did it. I know better than you.

Pam You usually touch your forehead.

> *Beat.*
> *Izzy touches her forehead with the tips of her fingers.*

Izzy And the mother slaps her hand.

> *Pam slaps Izzy's hand.*

Pam And the mother sighs and she gets quite cross because she knows about the sex but she can't say. Not that she minds but she still can't say, 'Go and get a drink of water. You don't drink enough water.'
Roslyn says, 'I don't like tap water.'

Izzy 'I don't like tap water.'

Pam And Cath gets crosser. The mother gets crosser. 'Don't talk nonsense. This is the best water in the world. The water we have here.'
And Cath goes and she runs the tap.
'Come here.'

Izzy Roslyn goes through to the kitchen and she bumps her arm on the door jamb on the way and she has to rub it but the mother doesn't see. And her arm hurts and that makes the girl have tears in her eyes but her mother doesn't see.

Pam That wasn't Roslyn, was it?

Izzy Be in the game.

Pam You hurt your own arm. Where did you hurt it?

Izzy It's just bruised, that's all.

Pam Come and I'll rub it better.

Izzy Play the game. Be in the game.

Pam Let me see your arm where you hurt it.

Izzy Please, Pam. Please.

Pam She's away in a dream, your mother. She's always there, I grant you that. Her body's there. Where the fuck's her mind, answer me that?

Izzy Play.

Pam Cath runs the water into the glass.
'It's good and cold.'
She holds the glass out to the girl.

Izzy Roslyn doesn't take it.

Pam 'Come with me to the gig,' she says.

Izzy 'Come with me to the gig.' Cath goes on holding it out.

Pam 'You drink this, for you'll get nothing else this day so help me. All your cucumbers and your creams. All your juices that I would have pressed for you. Your crispy potatoes. You'll get none of them. And your rail ticket, you can say goodbye to that. I won't open my purse this day. So help me God.'

Izzy And Roslyn just looks.

Pam 'Come and see the gig,' she says.

Izzy 'Come and see me sing.' 'How can I?' the mother says.

Pam 'How can I? I've twenty-seven members of the Women's Institute arriving at seven sharp wanting to be fed. I can't leave your father alone with that. Drink the water. Do you good.'

Izzy And then she's gentle. 'Drink the water, cherub,' Cath says.

Pam 'Drink the water, cherub.'

Izzy Gentler.

Pam 'Come on, my cherub.'

In the café.

Stuart Spanish princess.

Cath Me?

Stuart For your hair and your lips and the look in your yes.

Cath Jesus God, never trust a flatterer for they'll aye take you out to look at the moon.

Stuart Did your mother tell you that?

Cath I've looked at many a moon.
   It's rude to stare.

Stuart I'm not looking at you.

Cath Are you not?

Stuart I've a slight squint. I've had it from childhood. See. (*He stands up. Pulls her round to the light.*) The teasing I used to get in the playground. Children can be cruel.

Cath Your eyes look fine to me.

   She's caught looking into his eyes. He laughs.
      She refills the glasses.

Sadie and Ina are walking along the prom.

Ina You want me to be a landlady?

Sadie In a manner of speaking.

Ina Exactly what manner's that?

Sadie Eh?

Ina A boarding-house landlady?

Sadie A hotel.

Ina The landlady of a B and B.

Sadie An hotel, Ina. For God's sake, are you deaf?

Ina In Ilfracombe?

Sadie Woollacombe.

Ina Do I look like a landlady?

Sadie Proprietor, Ina.

Ina Proprietor? Proprietor! Is it a pub is it, that you need a proprietor? You'd put me to serve behind a public bar?

Sadie Only if you want to.

Ina I'm not a service industry, Sadie. I'm not now, I never was and I don't intend to be, not at any time in the future.

Sadie I'll tell you what you are, Ina.

Ina I'm always glad to learn something, Sadie.

Sadie You're a snob.

Ina There's not a damn thing wrong with that. (*Ina's unwrapping her chips.*)

Sadie Leave them, can you not? Leave them till we sit down.

Ina Oh my God. (*She holds up a chip.*)

Sadie What's wrong with you?

Ina Vinegar.

Sadie Vinegar?

Ina Look at that.

Sadie What am I looking at?

Ina That's a limp chip.

Sadie My God, Ina, I thought you'd been poisoned.

Ina It's anaemic, Sadie, you'll not deny that.
  You should have asked me.

Sadie Asked you?

Ina I don't like vinegar.

Sadie I assumed you did.

Ina Never assume anything, Sadie. It's very bad manners.

Sadie You were in the toilet. How am I supposed to ask.
Am I supposed to shout, am I?

Ina Don't be so damn stupid.

Sadie Well then.

Ina I know you like vinegar. I've always known that.
I don't assume. I don't have to. Just like I know you take
black tea. Tell me, Sadie. You tell me, I know your likes
and dislikes, how come you're so ignorant of mine?

Sadie Vinegar?

Ina I like salt.

Sadie Put them in the bin, I'll buy you some more.

Ina I'll do no such thing.

Sadie Give them to me.

Ina I'm not wasting good food.

Sadie I'll not have you eating something you don't like. Give them to me.

Ina I'm eating them.

Sadie I don't want you to. Give them to me. I'll buy you some more.

Ina I don't admire profligacy in a person. I never liked a show-off.

Sadie This was supposed to be a treat.

Ina It's no treat with vinegar on it.

Sadie For God's sake. I bought them, I paid for them, they're my chips, give them to me.

She puts Ina's fish and chips in the bin. Walks off.

Ina Yours'll be cold when you get to them. They're no treat cold.

Sadie chucks hers in the bin.

Sadie!

Sadie Will we start again? Will we? We'll get our fish and chips and we'll sit and we'll watch the sunset and we'll start again. I have plans, Ina. I want to share them with you.

Ina You'll do as you must. I can't stop you.

Corinne's in the distance. Ina watches her.

What's she expecting in that dress? What will she get? Eh? You answer me that.

Sadie I like it.

Ina Plenty salt.

Sadie Eh?

Ina No vinegar, Sadie. Plenty salt with my chips, if you please.

Stuart's looking at Cath.

Stuart You don't say much, do you?

Cath I live alone.

Stuart Don't get me wrong. I like quiet. Driving, you know. You get used to the quiet. A quiet woman though? Life's full of contradictions. A toast? To tranquillity? Eh?

> *Cath raises her glass.*

Cath Why not?

Izzy's watching Corinne.

Pam What is it?

Izzy Look at her.

Pam White's nice at night.

Izzy If you like that sort of thing.

Pam Uh-huh, well.

Izzy It's practically see-through.

Pam Only with the light behind it.

Izzy Would you wear that?

Pam I'm too . . . tall.

Izzy Could I wear it?

Pam Pretend Roslyn takes the glass of water and she throws it in the mother's face.

Izzy She didn't do that. She'd never have done that. They loved each other. That's why she's still sad, her mother. This whole year on, she's still sad.

Pam I've my mother's body. I look down sometimes and it's her I see. I'm not here at all. It's a nightmare, my mother's body.

Izzy Pretend Roslyn just thinks about throwing the glass of water in the mother's face but she drinks it instead.

Pam Pretend Roslyn gets cholera from it and that's how she dies this time.

Izzy Pretend she doesn't. She drinks the water.

Pam Her nose wrinkles and the mother sees it.
'Don't you pull that face.'
Roslyn says. 'You taste it.'

Izzy 'You taste it.'

Pam And the mother does.
And the mother dies of cholera.

Izzy How can she be dead, the mother? How can she be? There she is in her restaurant serving her food to that man. She can't be dead, can she?

Pam It's a game, Izzy.

Izzy You can't play that Roslyn lives. How can you play that? She won't come back to life, will she? No matter what we play. She'll still be torn and buried in the earth. Play real, Pam. It's got to be real. It only works if it's real.

Pam You don't know what 'real' is. Like your mother before you.

Izzy And you do, I suppose?

Pam Yes, I do, actually.

Beat.

Izzy The mother looks at her daughter. Cath looks at her daughter. 'I was brought up on this water,' she says. 'This is the best water in the world. It's got the sweetness of the rocks and the sweetness of the land in it. You drink that and the sweetness will enter into you. And it'll cure your ring of fire. And one day some man will see the sweetness in you and he'll taste it from your skin and he'll love you and he'll marry you.'

Pam That's stupid.

Izzy How is it?

Pam She never really said any of that. You just make it up.

Izzy's twisting her bracelet.

Izzy I hear it. You know I hear it.

Pam Well, I'm not saying it.

Izzy What do you want to say then? Pam?

Pam We never talk about anything proper, you and me. Can't we just talk.

In the café.

Stuart Can I see you in the morning?

Cath laughs.

Like sun from the clouds.

He puts his hand up and touches her mouth. Very lightly. Moves his hand away again.
Matt's head turns at the sound of Cath's laughter.

47

Pam The moon's over there and the sun's still in the sky.

Izzy Is this 'talk'?

Pam Don't you love hot nights?

Izzy There's beasties in the creeper.

Pam There's heat in the roof-felt still. Makes you feel . . .

Izzy What?

Pam There's not a breeze.

Izzy What's wrong with you?

Pam Lie on your back and the heat comes right through to your bones. The heat melts your bones.

Izzy Don't, Pam.

Pam The heat of the day, Izzy. You can feel it fading. Like it fades into you. Like it's all yours, the heat of the day. Like it belongs to you.

Izzy It's as well it's just me looking at you. Rolling around. Don't ever do it in public, Pam.

Pam This night. It can last for ever as far as I'm concerned. There'll never be another night like this.

   Beat.

Izzy This is where Roslyn says goodbye. She says goodbye to her mother, and her mother says, 'Be careful.'
   I'll go if you don't play.

Pam 'Be careful.'
   'Amn't I always?' Roslyn says.

Izzy 'Amn't I always?'

Pam 'I'll get you some Evian water.'

48

Izzy 'The DVD of *Ocean's Eleven*'s out. Will you get me that too?'

'Don't push your luck,' the mother says.

Pam 'Don't push your luck.' She puts her arm round her daughter. 'They'll love your songs. I am so proud of you.' And she says to her mother – you, you say it. Go on.

Izzy 'You're an old bag sometimes, do you know that? I still love you though. Don't wait up.'

But she always waited up, the mother, which Roslyn knew.

Pam Cath waited up and they'd talk when Roslyn came home and have crackers and Camembert cheese or sometimes goat's cheese if there'd been a delivery. And her mother would see her tucked safely in.

Izzy We sang 'Bye Bye, Blackbird' at her funeral, for it was her bedtime song when she was wee.

Pam Tell the funeral.

Izzy The whole congregation cried and the funeral director said he wished someone would do that for him, when he died. Sing him a lullaby. Cath said she wasn't having any minister standing there with sadness in his voice saying her daughter was a good girl and she did her best for her family and he knew that God would know that and give her a place in Heaven. Which hurt my father for it was quite inaccurate, he wouldn't have mentioned Heaven at all. So we read poems and she'd written some of them herself for song lyrics and people who knew her talked about her life, the ones that could get their words out through their sobs. That's what I'm going to have at my funeral and I've made my will so it's there in black and white. I won't have any damn minister mouthing words over me. Specially not my father, for he'll say I'm waiting in God's vestibule. He'll describe the tortures of Hell so it'll be clear by implication to the assembled congregation where he thinks I'm headed; where he thinks my sins'll bring me to. I'll have no flowers, of course, but all my friends have to carry a single lily. You can carry two.

Pam Thank you.

Izzy I pressed the lily I carried to hers in the *Macmillan Children's Encyclopedia* and the pollen made a yellow stain. My father leathered me when he found it.

Pam When I die I'll play in God's green meadows. My spirit will frolic. My spirit will be in Heaven and it'll frolic with God and all his angels.

Izzy When I die I'll roast on the devil's big iron spit all wrapped in a polythene bag to keep my juices in.

Pam And I'll see her there, Roslyn. She'll be a jewel in God's bright Heaven.

Izzy There's no God.

Pam My mother says there's a Heaven.

Izzy Your mother's a liar and you're a fool. Only a fool believes a liar. There's no Heaven but what we make ourselves on this earth. That's our joy and our sorrow. Matt took her up into the long grass. He took her up to the long grass at the quarry side, Matt did. He showed her Heaven. He showed her Heaven there alright.'

Pam What did she show him?

   Beat.

Izzy Want to play 'Heaven at the quarry side'?

Pam Not tonight. Play the game of the last farewell.

Izzy You be Matt.

Pam I don't want to be the boy.

Izzy It's the game.

Pam I'm always the boy. I have to look down sometimes just to check I haven't grown a fucking penis.

On the beach Matt lights a cigarette.
  Cath's laughing.

Cath Oh God, do you remember smoking?

Stuart Do you want one?

Cath Have you got one?

Stuart Here.

  In the light of the dry tree.

Cath Here's what you do. What I remember. From long ago I remember this. There's a man. You get a cigarette off him. You stand and wait till he strikes a match. You never take your eyes off him. You cup your hands round his as he holds the match to shield the flame. You take a light. You lean against him. You take a long drag. His arms go round you. You watch the moon on the water.

Stuart See now. There was a dry tree. And the Madonna. She passed by. And the tree bore fruit. And it was a miracle. (*He gives her a cigarette.*)

Cath It's only lanterns.

Stuart Spanish princess.

  He strikes a match. She cups his hands. Takes a light.

On the prom.

Ina You took your time.

Sadie There was a queue.

Ina You left me exposed. I was exposed again.

Sadie Are you going to take these?

Ina On your own, sitting. There's no loneness like it.
They all pass by. All the world looking. Thinking you've
got no friends. That's an awful thing. Poor soul, they
think. All alone on a long light night. What's she done
that she shouldn't have a friend? And then of course you
think. You can't stop it. Your mind presents things to you
and you have to look at them. When you're alone you
have to. You don't want to, but there's nothing to distract,
not when you're on your own. You have to pick over
what the mind throws up. You have to chew on it. I'm
thinking about the lilies that were on Bill's grave, Sadie.
The scent of those lilies caught me by the throat while I
was sitting here. I near choked on the scent of those lilies.

Sadie You can't smell them from here. Even with a wind
in the right direction.

Ina I'm an awful fool.
   It's been a woman with the lilies. All these years.
There's a woman puts flowers on my husband's grave.

Sadie I've your chips here, Ina, and a nice bit plaice.

Ina Plaice?

Sadie What's wrong with that?

Ina Did they not have cod?

Sadie I'm going to have mine.

Ina Is yours cod?

52

Sadie Mine has vinegar.

Ina Of course it's very nice of you.

Sadie Think nothing of it.

Ina I loved my husband, Sadie. The light of my life. He was all the world to me.

Sadie Eat that while it's hot.

Ina breaks a bit. Bites. Breathes in sharply. Pants.

What's wrong?

Ina I burnt my damn tongue, Sadie. What does it look like? My God, Sadie, all the way down that's burning me.

Izzy 'I've gone through a pipe,' Matt says. They're in front of the hotel. He's in his overalls that he's been lent. For it's the holidays and Cath gave him the job of stripping the upstairs hotel-room floors with a big sander thing. He looks nice in his overalls. And he's got them off on the top so they hang down from his waist. So his chest's bare. And he looks nice. Roslyn thinks he looks nice. Play.

Pam 'I've gone through a pipe. There's water pouring down through the ceiling. It's dripping through the fucking light. I can't leave it. The whole place could go up.'
    'Have you turned the electricity off?' Roslyn says.

Izzy 'Have you turned the electricity off?'

Pam 'Your mother's going to kill me.'

Izzy 'Look.' She's got this thing in her hand, Roslyn, and she holds it out flat on her palm. And it's silver and it's worn-looking like it's been loved and kept warm, the silver, by the heat of someone's body, by the heat of her body. And Matt looks at it. 'What's that for?' he says.

Sadie Is that good?

Ina Fills a hole.

Cath Back then I'd wear a silk slip and red red lipstick and stiletto shoes and have a man's hand push the slip up just gently, just slowly, push the slip up so the silk and the lace just crush against my thigh and the heat of his hand comes through onto my skin. And we'd be on the shore just where the waves are slow and they lap the stones in the last heat the day's got in it.

Stuart Stilettos on a stony beach.

Cath Maybe I'd take them off and I'd have them in my hand.

Pam 'What's that for?'

Izzy 'Keep you safe.'

Pam 'It's warm.'

Izzy puts the bracelet on Pam's wrist.

Izzy After Matt's kissed her – you kiss me.

A quick kiss.

Pam You can do better than that.

A longer kiss.

Izzy He runs his finger down the side of her cheek. Go on.

Pam runs her finger down the side of Izzy's cheek.

Matt says, 'Go in the car.'

Pam 'Why don't you go in the car? Go and take my place in the car.'

Izzy 'Do you want me to play the drums for you too?'

Pam 'That's sorted. Go in the car, go on.'

Izzy 'See, if you wear this we'll always be in touch. As long as you keep this on. So we will. Always.' Matt says he better get back to the water dripping through the light and the mess he's made going through the pipe with the sander. But he puts his arms round her. Roslyn puts her head on his shoulder just for a minute. She leans it there like she's his and he's hers for ever. (*Izzy puts her head on Pam's shoulder.*)

Pam Matt lights a cigarette and he puts it in Roslyn's mouth. (*She lights the cigarette.*)

Izzy And they stay there for a minute, like they've all the time in the world though she'll miss the car if she doesn't hurry, and the blue smoke rises into the air that's still hot from the sun. Last year. Last year's sun.

Pam 'I've nothing for you. I've never given you a present.'
'Plenty time,' Roslyn says.

Izzy 'Plenty time.'
We played the fucking funeral in the wrong place.

On the prom. Sadie chokes and chokes.

Ina Sadie? Sadie?

She claps Sadie on the back. Over and over.

God help me, God help me, Sadie. Is it a fish bone? What is it? Is it a fishbone, Sadie? Sadie?
Oh God. Oh my God.
I've some bread, Sadie. I've some bread here that I brought for the sea gulls. I've some bread here in my bag,

55

Sadie. Wait now. Wait while I get the bread. You swallow the bread, Sadie. Swallow the dry bread. What my mother always said. Here, Sadie. Here's a bit bread. You swallow it. Swallow it now. I always have bread for the gulls, Sadie. The way they wheel for the bread. I swear those gulls know me, Sadie. Flying in their great big circles. Swooping down to my hands, Sadie. You swallow that bread. Come on now. Swallow. Watch the gulls now, Sadie. See them. Didn't I tell you they know me when I get my bread out, Sadie. There now. There now. Gently now. See. See. My mother knew a thing or two. Whatever you think of her. They knew a thing or two in those days, Sadie.

Look at your eyes. Your poor eyes are streaming, Sadie.

The fright.

I thought I was losing you.

Sadie (*hoarse and heaving for breath*) My whole life flashed in front of me. And there wasn't much of it, Ina. There was so little of it. And I've a chance for more. And with the breath I couldn't catch, Ina, that chance fled from me.

Ina It means that much to you.

Cath's not looking at Stuart. Her voice is cool.

Cath There was a girl here, you know. She was killed. It's a year now. She had a gig in the town. The band were playing the songs she'd written. She was singing her own songs. First time ever. Imagine. Her standing there at the microphone. Her mother bought her the frock she was wearing. Her mother bought it specially. You can just see her, can't you? She's on her own in the light. One arm

56

behind her back, holding on to herself. The set's over. She's biting her lip. Then she sees. She sees how they all love what she's done. Just slowly she sees. And she smiles. The girl had a lovely smile. You'd want your child to have a bit like that in her life, wouldn't you?

Stuart You were there, I suppose?

Cath I was working.

On the prom.

Sadie I need a sherry.

Ina Eh?

Sadie We could have a sherry to us.

Ina Here?

Sadie Some sherry for my throat's rasping.

Ina When are you going? Are you going, when are you going? For you are going, aren't you?

Sadie There was a moment there when I certainly was. I was going a lot further than I thought, a lot faster and a hell of a lot sooner. That's how my mother died. Choking. My father used to hang her upside down. Then one day she choked and he wasn't there. She always said she'd do that. 'I depend on your father for life itself,' she said. I watched her. Nothing I could do. I just didn't have the height. Funny really.

I need a sherry. Dry sherry. Harvey's. A schooner. What do you say?

On the flat roof.

Pam I'm going to be her.

Izzy You are not.

Pam I've got the bracelet.

Izzy That's mine. Give it to me. Give me my bracelet.

Pam I get to be her.

Izzy Don't make me fight you for it.

Pam You're always her.

Izzy I'm the one can reach her. You just pretend.

Pam We're both fucking pretending. I'm up to here with this game.

Izzy You are not.

Pam I always have to be the men. And we never talk. And you're never you.

Izzy Come on, play.

Pam I'm done with it.

Izzy You are not.

Pam We're not even friends any more. Not friends.

Izzy Give me my bracelet.

Pam You're really fucking odd, do you know that? Everybody thinks so.

Izzy Give me my fucking bracelet, Pammy.

Pam Don't call me that.

Izzy Pammy. Pammy. Pammy.

Pam Roslyn got in the car after the gig thing in the town.

Izzy She doesn't die yet.

Pam They all got in the car, the band. And they were tired but they were happy because it had gone so well, the gig. Though the man from the record company hadn't turned up because they never do. Still, they were happy.

Izzy It isn't time yet.

Pam Roslyn was tired, she was really tired because she'd been so frightened. So she fell asleep which was fine because she wasn't driving, after all. It was the bassist who was driving. He had a five-string bass. That was in the boot. The guitarist, he fell asleep next. Then the one that did the sampler. Last of all to fall asleep was the bassist himself. It went over the central reservation, the car. And it took off as it went. She was thrown out the back, Roslyn. None of them knew anything about it, being asleep. So they didn't suffer. She was a broken doll on the road. And though there were fractures in many places it was her cut arm that killed her first. She remembers her mother touching her face in the mortuary. She remembers her mother stroking her hair.
   Look.

On the front Matt has his arms round Corinne and he puts a cigarette between her lips.

Izzy Give me my bracelet back.

Pam The way you follow Corinne. You always follow people. The way you followed Roslyn and Matt before. You haven't got a life of your own. You suck at other people's.

Izzy Please, Pam. Please give it back.

Pam Come and get it. (*She holds the bracelet far above her head.*)

Izzy You have to give it back.

Pam You suck your friends dry, too.

Izzy Give me my bracelet. Give me it. Give me it.

Pam chucks the bracelet in the sea.
   Beat.

Pam See now. See. I don't ever have to play the fucking game again. Do I?

   Beat.

Izzy. Izzy?

On the beach.

Matt You'd have liked her.

Corinne I don't want to fucking like her. I don't want ever to think of her. See up in the grass. When we're up in the grass. There's three of us there. I mean, how perverted is that? All the time we're there it's like she's watching us.

Matt I'm not thinking about her.

Corinne Yes you are. You are. She's pulling at you. I mean, that's fine. It's not like I don't understand her holding on to you. Shit, listen to me. It's you, for fuck sake. You're holding on to her.

She flicks the cigarette over the rail, watches it arc down to the sea.

Shite, Matt. You've got the bracelet even. You never take it off. You never ever take the fucking thing off. (*She walks away.*)

In the café.

Stuart All right now.

Cath stands there.

Hey, hey, hey. It's all right.

On the prom.

Ina Is that a schooner?

Sadie Things get smaller as you get older.

Ina How can you leave here? Look at that sun. Did you ever see such a sun. I never tire of this. If I didn't watch this, would it be here, do you think? Would it be here?

Sadie Drink your sherry.

Ina I've never sat on the prom on a warm night with a glass in my hand. Not when Bill was alive. Not even then. And he liked a drink. That's an awful thing.

Sadie I want you to come with me.

Ina Don't be ridiculous.

Sadie We've been friends a long time.

Ina What's that got to do with it?

Sadie We've been good friends.

Ina Of course we have.

Sadie It's only a small establishment, Ina. It's a dear place. You should see the folk that go there. Young folk go there.

Ina What would they want with you?

Sadie They want their beds clean. They want meals on the table. What do they care who puts them there?

Ina What do you know about running a hotel?

Sadie I can learn.

Ina That's your establishment. Over there in that churchyard. That's your next establishment. A coffin, Sadie. A coffin under a cold stone.

Sadie It faces the surf, Ina. The proper sea. Not this inlet we live upon. The surf pounds down on the beach. All the white horses.

Ina There's nothing wrong with this.

Sadie Some days there's a lull, then the boys get their guitars out.

Ina If it's guitars you want. You don't need to travel to find guitars, Sadie. We have plenty guitars of our own. We have Scottish guitars, Sadie. My own husband had a guitar. He had a Cromwell that a dealer offered me money for and I said no. That guitar hangs upon my wall. It hangs upon the wall in the house that I lived in with Bill. The house that I'll live in till the day I die. You come to my house, Sadie. You can stare at Bill's guitar. And in the cold, Sadie, you can hear the winter waves pound upon this beach. You get surf then. In the winter you get surf all right.

Sadie I didn't mean to frighten you.

Ina Get me another glass of sherry and you make it a schooner this time. I mean a proper schooner.

In the café.

Stuart Here. (*He offers her a piece of chewing gum.*)

Cath I'd rather have a cigarette.

> *He lights one for her. Chews gum. She watches him.*
> *Smokes.*

There was a little girl and her papa loved her very much
and she would chew chewing gum though her papa told
her not to for it could kill her. And one day it did kill her.
The chewing gum got caught in her gullet and she
couldn't breath for it blocked her windpipe and her papa
could do nothing but watch her die. And oh, he was very
sorrowful with his little granddaughter's big dying eyes
upon him. And her grandfather buried her. And on her
grave he put up a stone. And on the stone he carved these
words. With his own hand:

> Never chew, chewing gum,
> Chewing gum, chewing gum,
> Never chew chewing gum,
> For that's what brought me here.

I used to tell my daughter that like my papa told me,
back when people only died in stories.
    Right.

> *She stubs out the cigarette. Walks away. Turns.*

Strictly speaking, I should follow you. You should take
my hand gently. Look at it like it's one of God's miracles
and there's never been such a hand. Maybe kiss it. Grab
a bottle of champagne. Lead me to your room.

> *Walks away.*

But you don't know where it is, do you? You'll find the
ceiling's high. There was water damage. We had to
replace the plasterwork.

Stuart I like a nice bit of plasterwork. A nice ceiling rose. A ceiling rose can make a room.

The beach.
  Matt shouts.

Matt Hey.

Izzy Don't you fucking shout at me.

Matt What're you doing?

Izzy What does it look like?

Matt You can't go in there with your clothes on.

Izzy Why?

Matt You're too young.

Izzy There's an age requirement, is there, for getting your fucking clothes wet?

Matt What the fuck are you doing?

Izzy I'm drowning myself, actually.

Matt What for?

Izzy There's no fucking love in the world.

Matt Is that a fact?

Izzy You're shagging Corinne, aren't you?

Matt I'm not coming in there after you.

Izzy If you're shagging her tonight, try the roof outside her bedroom. The flat roofs keep the heat as it turns out. You'll be fine there if you don't mind the beasties in the creeper. They're all right on your skin, it's when you open your mouth and they fly in that it's not so very nice.

Matt I'll keep my mouth closed.

Izzy Is that supposed to be funny?

Matt Are you looking for something?

Izzy I'm the only one that remembers Roslyn.

Matt Who do you think you're talking to?

Izzy I've been keeping her alive.

Matt No you haven't.

    Beat.

Izzy See if living's being empty inside. See if it's being empty all the time. I don't want it. I won't have it.

    Matt lights a cigarette.

Don't smoke. Don't fucking smoke.

Matt Want a drag?

Izzy I know your game.

Matt Fair enough.

    He stands smoking, watching her.

Cath is standing in the middle of the bedroom.

Cath Of course if we hadn't put the bathroom in, the plaster would continue all the way round. And the ceiling rose would be central. As it is, it's quite off centre. Which is a pity.

Stuart I take your point.

Cath Still.

Stuart We could sit down.

Cath On the bed?

Stuart pulls out a chair.

Stuart Will that do you?

Beat.

We can talk if you like.

Cath It was fun down there.

Stuart We don't have to . . .

Cath No, no, no. We'll do it. We will. I want to. What's funny?

Stuart You don't exactly make it the most appealing thing in the world to contemplate.

Cath Women like me? You meet a lot of us?

Stuart Smell the honeysuckle?

Cath It's very bright still.

Stuart I could close the curtains.

Cath They're not that thick.

Stuart Nice curtains.

Cath D'you not hate that?

Stuart What?

Cath Daylight through the curtains?

Stuart I'll leave them open then.
It's only the last rays of the sun we're getting now.
You're a lovely woman.

Cath See that light.

Stuart It's ornate to say the least.

Cath Doesn't work.

The crash, the one the four kids were killed in. This light hasn't worked since that night. We've had electricians to see to it. The last one didn't even charge. Electrician was that puzzled. Said there was no reason on earth the light shouldn't work. It's been a whole year now since the crash. A whole year and that light hasn't switched on.

    Beat.

Funny.

Stuart Was that supposed to make me shiver pleasantly and celebrate the strangeness of the world?

    Beat.

Cath We should've painted this in an off-white. Maybe a tinge of rose. To catch the sunset colours.

Stuart Who's this 'we'?

Cath I've never been fond of yellow. I like a sunset. Better than a sunrise I like it.

On the beach.

Izzy I saw you once here with her. She was in the water and you waded in after her. And you picked her up in your arms. You didn't care that you got wet and you took her out of the sea and you laid her down over there.

Matt Bit of a voyeur, you.

Izzy Your skin's green in the moonlight.

Matt Olive surely?

Izzy I've lost my bracelet.

Matt Come here. (*He holds out his hand to her.*)

67

Izzy I need my bracelet.

Matt What for?

Izzy I need to find it.

Matt Don't go out of your depth.

Izzy I've got to find it.

Matt I'll give you a bracelet.

   Beat.

Izzy What do you mean?

Matt I've a bracelet you can have.

Izzy Don't be stupid.

Matt Come on, come here. Come and you can have it.

   He takes the bracelet off and holds it out to her.

Stuart lifts the edge of Cath's skirt. Pushes it up. Quite, quite delicately.
   He kisses her. They make love.

On the flat roof.

Izzy What?

Pam What?

Izzy I'm changing my name to Belle. Means beautiful.

Pam Means shite.

Izzy I'm going to be Belle from now on.

Pam You'll always be Izzy to me.

Izzy There he is. See. Do you?

Pam Uh-huh.

Izzy Do you, though?

Pam It's not like I've never seen him before.

Izzy There's five years between us.

Pam What about it?

Izzy It's perfect.

Corinne stands on the prom steps leaning on the iron banister.

Matt I thought you'd gone.

Corinne I was always taught not to waste good food.

Matt Want a sausage?

Corinne It's charcoal.

Matt It's lived a life, this sausage.

Corinne Hell of a life.

Matt There's potatoes still.

Corinne Lift me down then.

   He lifts her, holds her there.

Matt? (*She laughs.*)

Put me down.

Matt No.

Corinne Put me down now.

Matt Say please.

Corinne Please, for fuck sake.

Matt Smile when you say it.

Corinne Nothing to smile about.

He carries her down to the edge of the sea.

Matt You're going in there.

Corinne There's seaweed for God's sake.

Matt Say please and smile.

Corinne Never.

Matt carries her into the water.

You'll get soaked.

Matt So will you.

Dips her down to touch the water.
Corinne screams.

Corinne Jesus Christ, Matt, it's fucking freezing.
Don't you dare drop me.

Matt I loved her, right? Roslyn.

Corinne Don't drop me.

Matt I love the memory of her. I always will.

Corinne Matt?

Matt That's all she is.

Corinne A memory?

He kisses her.

Matt You're no lightweight, you know that.

Drops her. She screams. Splashes him. Runs out of the water up the beach. He chases, catches her. Holds her tight.

Ina slugs back some sherry, spilling a drop.

Ina Have you a hankie?

Sadie I'll take you home.

Ina I'm not drunk.

Sadie Did I say you were?

Ina It takes more than a couple of glasses of sherry.

Sadie I know.

Ina I've drunk whisky before now. I've drunk whisky and I've stood in the dawn and told the tale.

Sadie Hogmanay.

Ina We've seen a few of those.
   Why did you have to ask me?

Sadie I'm sorry.

Ina I was at peace, Sadie. You don't know what that is, do you? You never have.

Sadie I'll sell it if you don't come with me. I'll not do it on my own.

Ina You play dirty.

Sadie What are you talking about?

Ina If I don't come with you, you'll give it up?

Sadie What of it?

Ina Give it up that easy I don't think much of you. If a few words put you off, it didn't mean anything in the first place.

Sadie Will you come with me?

Ina As an unpaid skivvy?

Sadie Partner, Ina.

Ina You're too generous.

  Beat.

I was born here. I belong here. I'll die here. It's in my bones.

  If I stay you'll have something to come back to. If you close the establishment. If the business fails. I'll be your safety net, Sadie.

Sadie You've always been that.

Ina Take your hand off my arm. I'm not drunk.

Sadie Would you visit me?

Ina What would it do without me? The sky here. Would it change if I didn't watch it. Would the tide come in to the shore?

  See the tree at the back of my garden, it needs me there to watch its colours come and go.

  And the guitar, Sadie. Bill's guitar. Sometimes of a night in the winter when the central heating's on, I hear it. Just soft. Just the strings. What do you suppose that is, Sadie?

Sadie I don't know.

Ina I like to hear it.

Sadie You'd not even visit me. You'd not even do that?

Ina Was it a man that left you the place? Was it?

  Beat.

Sadie It was my son.

  Beat.

Ina That's an awful thing, your son dying before you.

Sadie I didn't know him.

Ina Did he have no progeny of his own to leave his fine hotel to?

Sadie He was a bachelor.

Ina That's very exotic.

Sadie He had a lover that I met.
   What would he have said, Bill, do you think?

Ina Bill?

Sadie If he knew I had a son of that kind. If he knew I had a son.

Ina My husband was always fond of you.

Sadie I would like to have known my son, Ina. I'd like him to have got in touch with me before he died. I've stood at the window and I've watched the visitors in the summer and I've wondered if one was him. I've always waited for him to come to me.

Ina Did he leave the lover something?

Sadie He wasn't a poor man, my son.

Ina Pity about the lilies.

Sadie I beg your pardon.

Ina When you go. When you're running your fine establishment. My husband will miss his lilies.

Matt pours whisky into the cup of a silver hip-flask.
Corinne kisses him. Takes the whisky.

Corinne Play for me.

Matt Do you not want these potatoes?

Corinne I want to get dry.

Matt Come on to the fire.

Corinne In a minute. (*She hands him the guitar.*) Go on.

  He strums.

Matt How's this? (*He plays.*)

Corinne It'll do.

  She dances.

Stuart and Cath lean at the window and listen.

Cath Smell the wood smoke.

The girls climb onto the roof. The sound of the guitar. They're watching Corinne.

Izzy Cow with a musket, my father says I am, as far as the dancing goes.

Pam There isn't a person alive who can't dance.

Izzy He'ld look at me like that. One day. Matt would. Wouldn't he? If I could dance he would.

Pam Come here.

Izzy What for?

Pam Come on. (*She holds out her arms.*) See, dancing. What it is. You let go. That's what I think. You just let go. See where you get to.

74

Izzy That's daft.

Pam Try it.

Izzy You'll laugh.

Pam Come and lean on me. You lean. And I'm – oh – whoever you want me to be, that's who I am.

Izzy leans against Pam.

Now let go. Let it all go.

The guitar plays. The girls dance. Twilight falls. The sun sets. Night comes.

The End.